iLoveCrabs Cookbook

Recipes Inspired by the Passion, Love and Taste of the Chesapeake

Recipes by Chef Jeremy Bricker
Photography by Tom Wenger

CREDITS
Chef/Recipes: Jeremy Bricker
Photographer/Food Stylist: Tom Wenger - tomwenger.com
Designer: Tom Wenger
Contributors: Curt & Jessica Engle, Rob Gundermann

Printed in the United States of America

Second Edition, May 2016
First Printing, October 2015

ISBN: 978-0-9968141-7-1

For more information about Harbour House Crabs, visit

www.iLoveCrabs.com

HARBOUR HOUSE
CRABS™
"Guaranteed fresh. Anywhere."
iLoveCrabs.com

Dedicated to
Gerald "Jerry" Engle
July 11, 1948 – July 5, 2013

Foreword

It's hard to beat Maryland Blue Crabs for all around appeal and versatility. One of the Chesapeake Bay's most delicious contributions to our American way of eating, they rank right up there on our hit parade of food favorites.

"iLoveCrabs" celebrates the passion of eating - and sharing -- one of the Bay's greatest offerings. From appetizers, to soups to main course meals -- Harbour House Crabs helps Americans celebrate the crab with these carefully crafted recipes -- accompanied by photographs you can almost taste. Simply put, they can't stop talking about crabs. Why should they? Feasting on crabs with family and friends --is one of life's greatest pleasures.

Thank you Jessica and Curt for opening up your heart -- and kitchen -- to give us an inside look into the passion of an American success story that Harbour House Crabs has become -- by simply sharing the three words -- "iLoveCrabs."

Rob Ziemba - a friend, a fan.

iLoveCrabs

If you ask a Marylander or anyone that has spent significant time on the Eastern Shore their answer will undoubtedly be "iLoveCrabs".

For centuries, Maryland has been synonymous with Blue Crabs and the wonderful way they bring family and friends together. A well-recognized and proud symbol across the state, images of the Maryland Blue Crab are present on signs, license plates, t-shirts and just about anywhere else you can envision.

The Chesapeake Blue Crab species, Callinectes Sapidus (Greek meaning beautiful savory swimmer), is celebrated for its mouth-watering sweet flavor that when steamed and seasoned becomes down right irresistible and a taste that many undeniably crave. With a little imagination or some favorite family recipes, the blue crab's savory meat can also be used to create many wonderful dishes. Fried, baked, steamed, broiled or whatever else you can think of has been tried to make many tantalizing Maryland favorites like jumbo lump crab cakes, soups, dips and more.

Each year Maryland residents and crab lovers from miles around gather at Maryland Crab Festivals throughout the spring, summer and fall to partake in the historic and rich tradition of the Crab Feast. While the taste is incredible, licking the seasoning off your fingers and chasing it down with your favorite cold beverage, the experience is truly unexplainable and something only those that have ever participated can appreciate. The smell of the spicy seasoning and seeing all the piles of steamed crabs fresh from the Chesapeake Bay spread all over the table makes you start salivating the moment you arrive.

Crab feast traditions are all about taking the time to slow down our busy lives and sit with family and friends while sharing memories. Not only are they about sharing memories and eating crabs but they are also about creating precious new memories that will last a lifetime.

iWantCrabs

For many Marylanders getting steamed blue crabs is as easy as getting pizza is for everyone else around the USA. They call or visit one of the many crab shacks located across the Chesapeake Region or some may even choose to catch and steam them on their own.

What do you do if you are landlocked like so many and not near the Chesapeake Bay area?

After relocating with his wife Jessica, only a short distance away from the region, Curt Engle found himself in this situation. He scoured the streets for the sweet, succulent flavor of the freshly steamed and seasoned Maryland Blue Crabs he enjoyed when boating.

Curt always had a love for the water and treasured all the enjoyable times spent on the Chesapeake Bay. His fondest memories were of the many Maryland Crab Feasts where he shared great times with his family and friends. Quickly realizing there was nowhere to get the taste he loved near his home and frustrated with his options, he decided to take matters into his own hands and Harbour House Crabs was born.

Starting with one store and quickly realizing there are crab lovers suffering all over the USA, they began taking orders online and delivering nationwide. The website name iLoveCrabs.com said it all. Catering to distant Maryland Crab lovers, the crabs are hand selected, perfectly seasoned and steamed to order the same day. Then packaged with care and shipped overnight anywhere in the country.

Now, nearly 20 years later, Harbour House Crabs is still a family owned and operated business and has grown beyond all expectations. "Guaranteed Fresh. Anywhere." is the promise Curt and his staff take great pride in meeting and exceeding for each delivery every day. Harbour House Crabs regularly receives heartwarming stories of how something as simple as the blue crab has brought family and friends together again to relive times from many years ago along the eastern shore.

Curt and Jess's goal was simple, help as many others to enjoy the unique taste and memorable experiences the Chesapeake has to offer and this cookbook is nothing more than a continuation of their passion.

HARBOURHOUSE
CRABS
WWW.ILOVECRABS.COM
(888) ILUV CRABS or (866) 428-6172

CONTENTS

Foreword   4
iLoveCrabs   5
iWantCrabs   6
How to Eat Crabs   10
How to Prepare Softshell Crabs for Cooking   12
How to Shuck Oysters   14

APPETIZERS

Cilantro Crab with Garden Vegetables and
Sweet Vinagrette   18
Blue Crab and Corn Salsa   20
Snow Crab Salad   22
Tarragon Lobster Salad   24
Clams Casino   26
Steamed Shrimp   28
Clams in Spicy Broth   30
Crab Bruschetta   32
Blue Crab and Corn Fritters   34
Sweet Balsamic Glazed Shrimp with Rosemary   36
Alaskan King Crab and Artichoke Heart Dip   38
Baked Blue Crab Dip   40
Mom's Crab Dip   42
Bacon Wrapped Lobster Bites   44
Stuffed Mushrooms   46
Panko Crusted Coconut Shrimp   48
Fire Shrimp   50
Broiled Shrimp Cocktail   52
Rosemary Shrimp Skewers   54

SOUPS

Ginger Crab Soup   58
Lobster Bisque   60
Maryland Crab Soup   62
She Crab Soup   64
Acorn Squash and Crab Chowder   66
Shrimp and Crab Corn Chowder   68
New England Clam Chowder   70

ENTRÉES

Dutch Oven Crabby Mac and Cheese   74
Steamed Blue Crabs   76
Broiled Lobster Tails   78
Blue Crab Marinara over Pasta   80
Blue Crab Risotto   82
Blue Crab, Artichoke Heart, and Sun Dried
Tomato Sauté   84
Alaskan King Crab Flat Bread Pizza   86
Seafood Wrapped in Pastry Dough   88
Roasted Garlic and Butter Blue Crabs   90
Shrimp Quesadilla   92
Alaskan Snow Crab and Vegetable Omelet   94
Jumbo Shrimp Scampi   96
Sautéed Soft Shell Crabs   98
Blue Crab Quiche   100
Jumbo Lump Crab Cakes   102
Fried Soft Shell Crabs   104
Lobster Newberg   106
Littleneck Clams with Chorizo   108
Jamaican Jerk Shrimp   110
Bricker's Cioppino   112
Baked Oyster Pie   114

SAUCES

Cocktail Sauce   118
Béchamel Sauce   118
Mornay Sauce   118
Hollandaise sauce   120
Remoulade Sauce   120
Spicy Honey Chipotle Sauce   120

DESSERTS

Espresso Brownie   124
Black Raspberry Cobbler   126
New York Style Cheesecake   128
Grasshopper Pie   130
Orange Sorbet   132
Fresh Mint Ice Cream   134

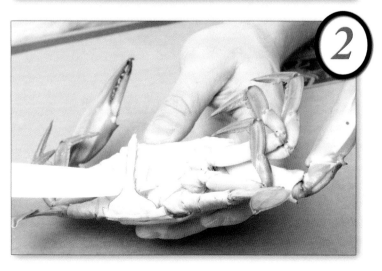

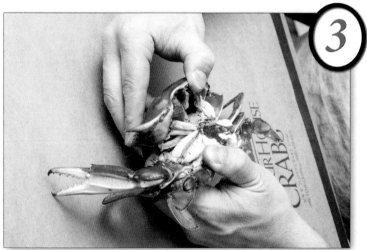

How To Eat Crabs

1) Size up your opponent - he's not so tough!
2) Place the crab on its back, belly up. Notice the apron in the middle of the crab's body. Use your fingers or a knife to lift up the apron. Pull it back away from the body, break it off and discard.
3) Turn the crab over, belly down and facing away from you. Lift up on the back of the shell and remove.

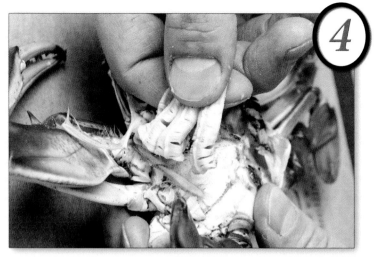

4) Next, with your fingers or knife, scrape off the six gills (lungs, sometimes referred to as the dead man's fingers) on both sides of the open body. These are not edible.

5) Remove the legs from the body retaining the pincher for later.

6) Break the crab in half so that you have a left side and a right side. The yellowish colored material found just behind the mouth area is the fat (mustard). Some people enjoy the taste of the "mustard" and some will pick it away.

7) Break each half in half again the opposite way, this will expose large clumps of meat that can easily be removed with your fingers.

8) Place the claw on the table with the claws facing up. Place a metal blade just behind the joint where the pincers join. Tap on the blade with a mallet, just enough to score the shell of the claw.

9) Using both hands, snap the claw in half removing a huge piece of claw meat.

10) You can either eat as you go or hoard a big pile. But hoarders must always protect their bounty from sneak attacks!

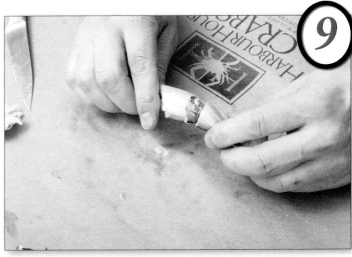

HOW TO PREPARE SOFT SHELL CRABS FOR COOKING

DIRECTIONS

• With kitchen scissors, cut the face side of the crab from the body thick enough to remove the eyes.

• Turn the crab over and pull up on the apron on the belly side and cut off.

• Turn the crab over again so the blue shell is facing up and lift the ends of the shell to reveal the lungs.

• Remove them also and you are now ready to cook your soft shell crab.

HOW TO SHUCK OYSTERS

The how-to on shucking fresh oysters. Feel free to add any flavoring you want when opened!

DIRECTIONS

- *Scrub the oysters with a stiff brush and rinse.*
- *Place the oyster on a towel in the palm of your hand to prevent cutting yourself.*
- *Work over a shallow bowl so you can catch the juices.*
- *Hold the oyster with the rounded side down and the flatter side up.*
- *One end of the oyster is rounded, and the other is hinged. Insert an oyster knife into the hinge, and twist. Some oysters are easier to open than others. If it is resistant, insert the oyster knife deeper into the hinge and twist.*
- *Finish opening the shell by using the oyster knife around the perimeter.*
- *Scrape down the bottom of the oyster to remove it from the grasp of the shell.*
- *Your oyster is now ready to be enjoyed!*

SIDES & APPETIZERS

CILANTRO CRAB WITH GARDEN VEGETABLES AND SWEET VINAIGRETTE

This is a cold salad best served as a starter coarse. The different flavors involved work really well together. The best way to start a meal! **SERVES 2-4**

DIRECTIONS

• Combine first 5 ingredients in a bowl, then put on separate plates.
• Mix the next four ingredients in a separate bowl and set aside. Make sure you gently fold in the crab meat.
• Blend the last four ingredients and drizzle on top of the vegetables.
• Place the crab meat mixture on top of the vegetables and serve.

INGREDIENTS

10 asparagus spears, cut in half (slightly cooked)

12 cherry tomatoes quartered

1 large shallot diced

1 orange pepper cut into 1 inch strips

1 japanese cucumber (peeled, seeded, and sliced)

1/4 cup non fat yogurt

Juice of 1 lime

1/4 cup fresh cilantro

1 cup jumbo lump crab meat

1/4 cup agave nectar

2 tablespoons balsamic vinegar

3 tablespoons extra virgin olive oil

Salt and pepper to taste

19

BLUE CRAB AND CORN SALSA

This salsa goes a long way. Serve it with tortilla chips or let it accompany your next meal. This will be gone before you know it! **SERVES 6-8**

DIRECTIONS

• Mix all ingredients in a bowl and serve!

INGREDIENTS

1⁄2 pound corn (thawed if frozen)

1⁄4 cup diced red pepper

1⁄4 cup diced green pepper

1⁄4 cup diced purple onion

3⁄4 cup diced roma tomatoes

2 tablespoons chopped garlic

1 teaspoon bay seasoning

1⁄4 teaspoon kosher salt

1⁄4 teaspoon black pepper

1⁄2 teaspoon crushed red pepper

Juice of 1 lime

Zest of 1 lime

1/3 cup fresh chopped cilantro

1⁄4 cup white vinegar

1⁄2 LB. jumbo lump crab meat

SNOW CRAB SALAD

A sweet, easy to make salad for your next party. This goes very well with tortilla chips or toasted bread. Just make sure you have a lot on hand, as this will be the first thing to disappear from your table. **SERVES 2-4**

DIRECTIONS

• Steam the snow crab legs and pick the meat, discarding the shells.
• Let the crab meat cool and mix all of the remaining ingredients in a bowl.
• Shred the crab meat with your hands and lightly fold in the chilled crab meat.

INGREDIENTS

2 1/2 lbs snow crab legs

Pinch of black pepper

1 tablespoon diced red onion

1 1/2 tablespoon diced green pepper

1 1/2 tablespoon diced carrots

20 small cherry tomatoes (quartered)

1 teaspoon bay seasoning

1 tablespoon white vinegar

1/2 cup mayonnaise

TARRAGON LOBSTER SALAD

You will be surprised at the sweetness of the lobster and the power of the tarragon in this recipe. The recipe calls for companelle pasta, but feel free to substitute with whatever pasta you have on hand. **SERVES 4-6**

DIRECTIONS

- *Blend all ingredients except pasta together and chill.*
- *Cook pasta until al dente and cool down.*
- *Toss mixture with pasta and serve.*

INGREDIENTS

1 large shallot diced

Juice of 1 lemon

1/3 cup mayonnaise

Pinch crushed red pepper

2 tablespoons chopped fresh tarragon leaves

Salt and black pepper to taste

2 cups of cooked lobster meat (24-28 oz. tail) cubed

1 teaspoon chopped garlic

1 cup companelle pasta

CLAMS CASINO

Littleneck clams work great, but a larger clam will do. **SERVES 2-4**

DIRECTIONS

• Place the bacon in a large sauté pan and cook on medium high heat until the bacon is cooked through.
• Add the vegetables, garlic, and butter and cook until the onion is clear, stirring often.
• Pour in the brandy and sprinkle with black pepper.
• Stir in the bread crumbs until well coated.
• Shuck the clams on the 1/2 shell, and scrape the sides until the clam comes loose, and place on a sheet pan.
• Top loosened clam with the casino mix.
• Bake in an oven at 350 degrees for 20 minutes.
• Take the clams out and sprinkle with parmesan and bread crumbs.
• Switch the oven to broil and place the tray back in for 2 minutes before serving.

INGREDIENTS

6 strips bacon

3/4 cup diced purple onion

1 cup diced green pepper

1 tablespoon chopped garlic

Black pepper to taste

2 teaspoons brandy

1/2 cup bread crumbs

3 tablespoons butter

24 top neck clams (shucked)

Parmesan cheese

STEAMED SHRIMP

This is a go-to recipe for steamed shrimp. The mace gives the shrimp a heavenly aroma and a hint of flavor. Serve hot or chilled with cocktail sauce and lemon wedges. **SERVES 2-4**

DIRECTIONS

• In a steamer pot, add all the ingredients except the shrimp, bay seasoning, and lemon.
• Let the liquid come to a boil.
• In the steamer pan, add the shrimp and season with bay seasoning as heavy or light as you want.
• Place the steamer pan in the pot, making sure it does not touch the liquid.
• Cover and steam for 10-15 minutes or until pink and cooked through.
• Take out of the steamer and serve hot or chill in the refrigerator.

INGREDIENTS

1 pound 16/20 jumbo shrimp

1 can light beer

2 bay leaves

1/4 teaspoon white pepper

1/4 teaspoon mace

1 teaspoon dried thyme

Bay seasoning

Lemon

CLAMS IN SPICY BROTH

It's easy and oh so good to scoop up the broth with your clams. You can freeze the extra liquid for another day! **SERVES 4-6**

DIRECTIONS

• Put all ingredients into a pot over medium heat and cover.
• Stir after 15 minutes.
• When all the clams are open, they are done.
• Place clams into a bowl and pour liquid over them.

INGREDIENTS

50 little neck clams

1 lemon quartered

1 lime quartered

1 stick of unsalted butter

1 tablespoon chopped garlic

1⁄2 teaspoon crushed red pepper

1/3 cup chopped jalapeño pepper

1 teaspoon bay seasoning

1/3 cup white wine

1⁄2 teaspoon white vinegar

1⁄4 teaspoon white pepper

CRAB BRUSCHETTA

This is a favorite side dish for any party. But you don't have to stop there. Top off some chicken or any other type of meat for a real treat. Simple to make and don't forget the toasted bread! **SERVES 3-4**

DIRECTIONS

• Combine all the ingredients except crab in a bowl and mix well.
• Gently fold in the crab meat.
• Serve with a drizzle of balsamic reduction on top if preferred.

INGREDIENTS

14 diced roma tomatoes

1 tablespoon fresh chopped garlic

1/3 cup fresh chopped basil

1/2 diced purple onion

1 LB. backfin crab meat

2 teaspoons bay seasoning

Salt and pepper to taste

Balsamic reduction (optional)

BLUE CRAB AND CORN FRITTERS

Exploding with flavor, these will have you hooked in no time. Fried to perfection, the sweetness of the corn pairs well with the crab. Try with our remoulade sauce (p.120) or be bold and go for the spicy honey chipotle sauce (p. 120). You wont be disappointed! **SERVES 4-6**

DIRECTIONS

• In a large pot, add about 6 inches of canola oil or use a home fryer according to its instructions.
• Heat until the oil reaches 340 degrees.
• Mix the top portion of the ingredients in a bowl and set aside.
• Mix the bottom portion of the ingredients in a separate bowl until well mixed.
• Add them both together to form a paste.
• Drop one tablespoon of the mixture at a time into the hot oil, making sure you do not overcrowd.
• Cook and rotate until golden brown (7-10 minutes).
• Remove from the oil and drain on paper towels.
• Repeat until all of the fritters are cooked.

INGREDIENTS

1 cup diced white onion

2 cups corn (thawed if frozen)

1/4 cup diced roasted red peppers

3 jalapeños seeded and chopped

1 teaspoon black pepper

1/2 teaspoon salt

2 tablespoons bay seasoning

1/4 teaspoon smoked paprika

----

1 1/2 LB backfin crab meat

3 eggs

Juice of 1 lemon

1 pint milk

1 tablespoon baking powder

6 cups flour

Canola oil

SWEET BALSAMIC GLAZED SHRIMP WITH ROSEMARY

This simple recipe is a family favorite! The sweetness of the shrimp combined with the balsamic vinegar is what sets these shrimp apart from the rest. The rosemary adds even more enticement. **SERVES 2**

DIRECTIONS

- Peel and devein the shrimp.
- Combine all ingredients in a heavy skillet over medium high heat.
- Flip the shrimp every 2 minutes.
- The sauce will start to get bubbly and the shrimp glazed. About 15 minutes.
- Remove from the heat and stir until well coated
- Move to a plate and serve

INGREDIENTS

1/4 cup balsamic vinegar

2 tablespoons brown sugar

2 oz. fresh rosemary

12 large shrimp (16-20 ct.)

ALASKAN KING CRAB AND ARTICHOKE DIP

What a delightful dip for any occasion! The sweetness of the crab balances well with the artichoke. Best baked and topped with panko crumbs. **SERVES 4-6**

DIRECTIONS

- Preheat oven to 350 degrees.
- Fold everything together except the king crab.
- Gently fold in the king crab.
- Place the mixture into an oven ready container.
- Sprinkle the panko bread crumbs on top and bake for 15 minutes or until bubbly.
- Serve with your favorite crackers or toasted bread.

INGREDIENTS

1 can (8.5 oz.) artichoke hearts (sliced)

1 red pepper diced

Salt and pepper to taste

2 large shallots diced

1 tablespoon bay seasoning

Juice of one lemon

2 8 oz. packets of cream cheese at room temperature

1/2 cup mayonnaise

3 cups cooked and shredded king crab legs (about 4 lbs.)

Panko bread crumbs

BAKED BLUE CRAB DIP

Another one of our favorite dips, This one has more of the crabby flavor we all love. **SERVES 4-6**

DIRECTIONS

• Preheat oven to 350 degrees.
• Mix first 8 ingredients together
• Place into a oven ready container
• Mix the last 3 ingredients together and spread evenly over the crab mixture.
• Bake for about 15 minutes or until it is bubbly and the topping is a golden brown.

INGREDIENTS

1/2 LB. jumbo lump crab meat

3/4 cup diced red pepper

1/2 cup parsley

1/4 cup chopped chives

Juice of one lemon

3/4 cup mayonnaise

1 teaspoon smoked chipotle Tabasco sauce

4 oz. packet of cream cheese (room temperature)

2 tablespoons melted butter

1/4 cup bread crumbs

1/4 cup parmigiana-reggiano cheese

MOM'S CRAB DIP

A delicious and simple dip recipe. It works very well to keep this heated in a small crock-pot. **SERVES 4-6**

DIRECTIONS

• Mix all but the crab meat in a double boiler and heat for 15 minutes, stirring often.
• Add the crab meat and keep warm.

INGREDIENTS

1 LB. crab meat (backfin)

2 8oz. cream cheese (softened)

2/3 cup Miracle Whip

1 teaspoon mustard

3 tablespoons chopped white onion

1 tablespoon 10x sugar

Garlic salt to taste

BACON WRAPPED
LOBSTER BITES

This is a perfect finger food. Bacon and lobster in the same sentence is a dream that becomes reality when you whip this recipe together. Perfect when topped with our hollandaise sauce (p. 120). **SERVES 2-3**

DIRECTIONS

• In a heavy skillet, cook the bacon in batches so it's not overcrowded.
• Lightly coat the bacon with the pepper while cooking.
• Remove from pan when bacon is done, not too crispy.
• Let rest on paper towels.
• Wipe out the pan and drain the juices.
• Remove the meat from the raw lobster tail and cut into cubes.
• Add the lemon, dill, and butter to the pan on medium high heat.
• Once the butter is melted, add the lobster.
• Stir every minute until the lobster is cooked through and golden brown (7-10 minutes)
• Take off heat and stir with the leftover pan juices.
• Wrap bacon around the lobster bites and place a toothpick in each one to hold the bacon
• Wipe out pan again, and heat on high heat.
• Add the bacon wrapped lobster bites to the pan and lightly sauté for 3-5 minutes until the bacon is heated.
• Best served topped with hollandaise sauce (p. 120).

INGREDIENTS

8 Slices apple-wood smoked bacon (cut in half)

Black pepper to taste

1 tablespoon clarified butter

1 tablespoon fresh chopped dill

Juice of 1 lemon

1 24-28 oz. lobster tail

45

STUFFED MUSHROOMS

These top-shelf stuffed mushrooms have no filler in them, and just the right amount of flavor. Top with our mornay sauce (p. 118) for a special treat.
SERVES 3-4

DIRECTIONS

- Clean the mushrooms and remove the stems.
- Pick the sorrel leaves and cut into thin strips.
- Mix in all the ingredients except the mushrooms and butter.
- Smoothly break up the crab meat while mixing.
- Fill the mushroom caps with the stuffing.
- Top with melted butter
- Bake at 350 degrees for 20 minutes

INGREDIENTS

.75 oz. package of sorrel (herb)

1 tablespoon chopped garlic

1/2 tablespoon lemon juice

1/2 LB. jumbo lump crab meat

1/2 teaspoon bay seasoning

Small pinch crushed red pepper

6-8 large silver dollar mushrooms

Melted butter

PANKO CRUSTED COCONUT SHRIMP

A tropical treat! The sweetness of the coconut and the crunchy panko bread crumbs do wonders for the shrimp. Enjoy with some lime. A simple recipe with a lot of steps. The only question is how much do you want to make?

DIRECTIONS

- Preheat a deep fryer to 340 degrees.
- Split the shrimp in half so only the inner curved edge is attached. This will make the shrimp long.
- In separate bowls, have your egg, flour, coconut, and panko.
- Coat the shrimp in the flour.
- Next the egg.
- Next the coconut.
- Next the egg again.
- Finally the panko.
- Be sure to fully cover with each ingredient.
- The best way to approach this is a little at a time, replacing the coconut and panko from time to time so they coat evenly with no clumps.
- Place 2-3 in the fryer at a time and flip them as they are floating for about 5 minutes or until golden brown.
- Remove from the fryer and set on paper towels to drain.
- Repeat steps until all your shrimp are done.

INGREDIENTS

Peeled and deveined shrimp with the tails on (16/20 ct.)

Flour

Egg

Coconut

Panko bread crumbs (plain)

FIRE SHRIMP

Where does the name come from? Maybe the flavor, but the "burnt" appearance is the actual source. This is a simple recipe that is packed with flavor. These are great on salads or all alone. **SERVES 2-3**

DIRECTIONS

- Heat the oil in a sauté pan over medium high heat.
- Add the shrimp and paprika and cook 4 minutes.
- Flip the shrimp over and add the butter.
- Cook another 4 minutes on high heat.

INGREDIENTS

1 teaspoon olive oil

1 tablespoon smoked paprika (more if desired)

1 tablespoon unsalted butter

12 peeled and deveined shrimp (16-20 ct.)

BROILED SHRIMP COCKTAIL

The secret behind this recipe is to brine the shrimp first. The "snap" of the shrimp is exactly what you crave. Delicious served with our cocktail sauce (p. 118).
SERVES 2

DIRECTIONS

- Mix the salt and sugar with the boiling water.
- Pour into a bowl with the ice and add the shrimp.
- Immediately place into your refrigerator for at least an hour.
- Set oven to broil.
- Take shrimp out of brine mixture and wash, then pat dry.
- Place shrimp on cookie sheet and drizzle with lemon juice and sprinkle with the olive oil.
- Cook 2 minutes each side.
- Place shrimp in refrigerator until chilled before serving.

INGREDIENTS

1/4 cup kosher salt

1/4 cup sugar

1 cup boiling water

2 cups ice

Extra virgin olive oil

Juice of 1/2 lemon

12 jumbo shrimp (16/20 ct.) Peeled and deveined, tail on

ROSEMARY SHRIMP SKEWERS

The citrus of the marinade and the rosemary complement each other perfectly. Serve these at your next bar-b-que for a real treat. **SERVES 2-4**

DIRECTIONS

• Mix all the ingredients together except for the rosemary.
• Place in the refrigerator and let sit for a couple of hours.
• Take your whole sticks of rosemary and skewer the shrimp. About 3 per skewer.
• Grill over medium heat for about 3 minutes each side.

INGREDIENTS

1 3⁄4 cup orange juice

1⁄2 cup lemon juice

1⁄2 teaspoon crushed red pepper

Pinch of salt and pepper

1⁄2 teaspoon smoked paprika

1 teaspoon chopped garlic

1 LB. Peeled and deveined shrimp (16-20 ct.)

Fresh rosemary

SOUPS

GINGER CRAB SOUP

A hint of ginger and a touch of ingredients that would never have been thought to be combined. This soup ends up being perfectly balanced.
SERVES 4-6

DIRECTIONS

• Add the butter, fennel, and ginger in a large stock pot over medium high heat.
• Stir until the butter is melted.
• Add the sweet potato and water and boil until the potatoes are cooked through.
• Add the artichoke hearts and blend with an immersion blender until smooth.
• Add the rest of the ingredients and simmer for about 25 minutes or until hot.

INGREDIENTS

1 stick of unsalted butter

1 sweet potato (peeled and cubed)

1/3 cup chopped fennel bulb

1/4 cup fresh ginger (peeled and chopped)

2 1/4 cups water

1 14 oz. can artichoke hearts

1/2 cup sliced scallions

2/3 cup diced roasted red peppers

2/3 cup chopped chicory leaves

1 lb. jumbo lump crab meat

1 cup half & half

Salt and pepper to taste

1/4 teaspoon bay seasoning

LOBSTER BISQUE

The soup that rivals the best. The work pays off in the end! **SERVES 4-6**

DIRECTIONS

• Fill a large stock pot with 1 1/2 inches water and place on high heat.
• Once the water starts to boil, add the teaspoon of salt and the lobsters and cover for about 15 minutes or until they are bright orange.
• Remove the lobsters from the pot, keeping the liquid in the pot.
• Take the meat out of the tail and the claws, and clean the body part of the lobsters, discarding their inner parts but keeping the shells.
• Over medium heat return the shells and a stick of butter to the same pan with the remaining liquid and cook for 5-10 minutes.
• Add 5 cups water and let simmer, covered, for 30 minutes.
• Drain the liquid through a colander into a bowl and discard shells.
• In a large sauce pan, add 1 stick of butter, the chopped onion and garlic on low heat until the onion is softened. (15 minutes).
• Add the flour and stir to make a roux.
• Add the thyme, wine, 2 bay leaves, and lobster broth.
• Simmer for 10 minutes.
• Chop the lobster meat and add into the pan and simmer another 5 minutes.
• Remove the bay leaves.
• With an immersion blender, blend until smooth (if using a regular blender, blend a little at a time so the blender does not overflow).
• Add the heavy cream and the sherry and simmer another 10 minutes, stirring constantly.
• Salt and pepper to taste.

INGREDIENTS

2 lobsters (1 1/2 lb. each)

2 sticks of unsalted butter

1 teaspoon salt

Salt and pepper to taste

1 medium chopped onion

1 tablespoon garlic

1/3 cup flour

1/2 tablespoon fresh chopped thyme

1 cup white wine

2 bay leaves

1/2 cup heavy cream

2 tablespoons sherry

61

MARYLAND CRAB SOUP

In Maryland this is the soup everyone talks about and it's hard to get out of the state without giving this one a try. Fresh blue crab, vegetables, with that bite of bay seasoning. How could you possibly go wrong? **SERVES 4-6**

DIRECTIONS

• Melt butter in a heavy cooking pot.
• Add the scallions, corn, cherry tomatoes, garlic, 2 tablespoons of the bay seasoning and mixed vegetables.
• Cook on medium high heat stirring occasionally until tomatoes are soft and can be crushed with a wooden spoon.
• Stir in the can of diced tomatoes and cover the pot until it reaches a slow boil.
• Add the water, claw meat, parsley, and 2 tablespoons bay seasoning.
• Let simmer, uncovered, for 30 minutes.

INGREDIENTS

1⁄2 cup clarified butter

2 cups scallions

4 ears of corn (husked and kernels taken off)

1 10.5 oz. cherry tomatoes

1 Tablespoon fresh chopped garlic

1 cup frozen mixed vegetables

4 tablespoons bay seasoning

1 28 oz. can diced tomatoes

3⁄4 cup fresh chopped parsley

4 cups water

1 LB. claw meat

63

SHE CRAB SOUP

A lot of patience goes a long way with this soup. The reward is unmatched. You can steam the crabs ahead of time, and then clean them, but cleaning them while alive and just before cooking will produce a fresher roe.
SERVES 2-3

DIRECTIONS

• Steam and clean the crabs, or clean the crabs when alive, saving the roe that is inside.
• Pick the crabs until all the meat is separated, place in a bowl with the roe and set aside.
• In a medium soup pan, add the butter and shallots and sauté until the shallots are tender.
• Add the flour and mix well to make a roux.
• Slowly mix in the milk and half & half on medium heat until thickened and the milk is hot.
• Bring to a slow simmer and add the rest of the ingredients until smoothly blended.
• A dollop of roe can be saved and used as a garnish.

INGREDIENTS

12 female crabs

3 tablespoons unsalted butter

1/3 cup minced shallots

2 heaping tablespoons flour

2 cups half and half

1 1/4 cup whole milk

1/2 teaspoon Worcestershire

1/4 teaspoon ground mace

1/4 teaspoon cayenne pepper

1/2 teaspoon grated lemon zest

1 tablespoon sherry

ACORN SQUASH AND CRAB CHOWDER

This is the perfect soup for fall when the crabs are coming in nice and heavy and acorn squash is plentiful. It's a real treat on those cool nights when you're wishing it was summer again. **SERVES 3-4**

DIRECTIONS

• In a large soup pot, heat the butter and oil over medium heat until the butter is melted.
• Add all the ingredients except the water, milk, bay seasoning, and crab meat.
• Stir constantly over medium high heat until the acorn squash is soft.
• Add the water and juice of one lemon and let it come to a boil.
• Use an immersion blender (or regular blender) to make a puree
• Thicken with cornstarch by mixing cornstarch with a little bit of water to make a paste, and add it into the puree until it is nice and thick.
• Add the milk, bay seasoning, and crab meat.
• Bring it down to a simmer for 15 minutes.

INGREDIENTS

1 tablespoon unsalted butter

1/3 cup extra virgin olive oil

2 acorn squash (peeled, seeded, and cubed)

3 small sliced shallots

1 medium white onion (sliced)

2 cups corn (frozen)

1 teaspoon minced garlic

1⁄2 teaspoon crushed red pepper

1 teaspoon rosemary

1 teaspoon thyme

1 tablespoon ground ginger

1 tablespoon smoked paprika

6 cups water

1 lemon

Cornstarch to thicken

1 pint whole milk

1 teaspoon bay seasoning

1 LB. crab meat

SHRIMP AND CRAB CORN CHOWDER

This hearty chowder is sure to be a crowd pleaser leaving your guests disappointed when they see the bottom of their bowls. **SERVES 4-6**

DIRECTIONS

- In a large soup pan, add the first five ingredients.
- Sauté on medium high heat until the corn starts to "crackle" and the onions are clear.
- Add the flour, Brie, and half & half.
- Stir until the Brie is melted.
- Next add the shrimp and heavy cream and let simmer for about 3 minutes.
- Pour in the water and cover, stirring occasionally until the shrimp are nice and pink.
- Add the bay seasoning, parsley, and crab meat.
- Stir and let simmer 5 minutes.

INGREDIENTS

4 ears of corn (2 1/4 cup)

1 stick unsalted butter

Pinch crushed red pepper

1/2 teaspoon ginger

1 small chopped white onion

2/3 cup flour

1/2 cup sliced Brie cheese (skinned)

1 cup half & half

1/2 cup heavy cream

15 peeled and deveined 16/20 jumbo shrimp (chopped)

2 cups water

1/2 teaspoon bay seasoning

1 teaspoon parsley

1/2 pound jumbo lump crab meat

69

NEW ENGLAND CLAM CHOWDER

The perfect soup for the clam lover. Rich and creamy, a must have for a dreary day. Of course any day will be perfectly fine! Once you have tasted it, you will appreciate the time involved. **SERVES 2-3**

DIRECTIONS

• In a heavy large pot, add the clarified butter, white wine, and clams.
• Cover on high heat until the clams open.
• Pick out the clams and place in a bowl.
• Once cooled, pick out the meat and discard the shells.
• Chop the clams until tender.
• With the left over juices, add the potatoes and cook until cooked through, yet firm. (10-15 minutes).
• Drain the potatoes and wash with cold water until cool.
• In the pot, cook the shallots, garlic, unsalted butter, rosemary and thyme for 5 minutes or until the shallots are tender.
• Add the flour and stir to make a roux.
• Stir in the heavy cream, milk, and clam juice on medium heat.
• Bring to a simmer while constantly stirring.
• Once it simmers, add the chopped clams, potatoes, and parsley.
• Turn off the heat and let it sit for 20 minutes before serving.
• Stir and add salt and pepper to taste.

INGREDIENTS

50 littleneck clams (washed and scrubbed)

1/4 cup white wine

4 tablespoons clarified butter

2 large shallots (chopped)

1 tablespoon chopped fresh garlic

3 baby gold potatoes (diced in 1/2 inch cubes)

1 cup unsalted butter (2 sticks)

1 teaspoon dried rosemary

1 teaspoon dried thyme

1 1/4 cup flour

3 cups whole milk

1 pint heavy cream

2 8 oz. jars clam juice

1/4 cup fresh parsley (chopped)

Salt and pepper to taste

ENTRÉES

DUTCH OVEN CRABBY MAC & CHEESE

This kids meal gets an adult treatment. But the kids will love it too (if you let them near it). **SERVES 6-8**

DIRECTIONS

- Preheat oven to 350 degrees.
- Cook pasta until very al dente.
- Sauté jalapeños, shallots and bacon in hot dutch oven until bacon is crispy stirring constantly, adding 1 tablespoon of butter when the bacon is about half cooked.
- Add milk and half and half and bring to a simmer.
- Add cheeses 1 cup at a time stirring constantly until all is melted.
- Add parsley, pasta and crab and lightly fold together.
- Bake in the oven for 1 hour or until the middle is firm.
- Sprinkle with bay seasoning when serving.

INGREDIENTS

1 LB. penne pasta

2 jalapeños (seeded and diced)

2 Shallots (diced)

1/3 cup maple bacon

1 1/2 cup milk

1 cup half and half

1 cup smoked mozzarella (diced)

1 cup smoked cheddar cheese (diced)

1 cup Gruyère cheese (diced)

1 cup smoked Gouda (diced)

1/4 cup fresh parsley (chopped)

1 teaspoon bay seasoning

1 1/2 LB jumbo lump meat

STEAMED BLUE CRABS

There are a lot of variations on how to steam crabs. Feel free to add any liquid or seasoning to this. This is our favorite though. **SERVES 6-8**

DIRECTIONS

• In a large stockpot, bring 1/2 cup bay seasoning, garlic, beer, lemons, and vinegar to a rolling boil.
• Fit either a screen or colander over the liquid so the crabs do not touch the liquid.
• Place in half the crabs and sprinkle 1/2 cup bay seasoning on the live crabs.
• Place the other half of the crabs on top and the rest of the bay seasoning.
• Cover and steam for at least 20-30 minutes or until all the crabs are bright orange and some of the fat is coming through the shell.

INGREDIENTS

3 dozen live crabs

1 1/2 cup bay seasoning

3 Beers (light or a lager)

2 cups apple cider vinegar

3 lemons sliced

1 bulb garlic

BROILED LOBSTER TAILS

A simple and effective way to broil lobster tails. **SERVES 2**

DIRECTIONS

• Turn broiler on and place the rack at the lowest level.
• Place the lobster tails on a sheet tray and fan out the fins.
• Cover the fins with leaf lettuce or loosely with aluminum foil so they do not burn.
• With scissors, cut down the middle of the lobster tail to the fin.
• Gently spread the shells apart and pull out the meat so it sits atop of the shells.
• Cut a small slit down the middle of the meat and spread the meat open to make a valley.
• Melt butter in separate pan.
• Cover with the melted butter, lemon, and paprika.
• Broil for 10-15 minutes or until golden brown and the center reaches 145 degrees.
• Add more lemon if desired.

INGREDIENTS

2 lobster tails

1 stick of unsalted butter

1/4 teaspoon paprika

Juice of 1 lemon

BLUE CRAB MARINARA

Simple and rustic, the flavors of this will definitely be a hit at the dinner table. You can serve this with a wide variety of pasta. **SERVES 2-4**

DIRECTIONS

- Heat oil in a large sauté pan.
- Add the tomatoes and onion on medium high heat, flipping the tomatoes in 5 minute intervals until they become soft.
- Crush the tomatoes with a wooden spoon.
- Add the rest of the ingredients except crab meat and simmer for 15-20 minutes.
- Gently fold in the crab meat and heat for another two minutes before serving.

INGREDIENTS

2 tablespoons extra virgin olive oil

4 heirloom tomatoes

1 medium sliced onion

1/4 cup fresh chopped basil

1 tablespoon chopped garlic

1 teaspoon lemon juice

1/4 teaspoon vanilla extract

1 1/2 teaspoon bay seasoning

1 tablespoon tomato paste

1 LB. jumbo lump crab meat

81

BLUE CRAB RISOTTO

Best served with pretty much anything or all on its own. **SERVES 4-6**

DIRECTIONS

• In a large sauté pan, melt 3 tablespoons butter with the shallots until the butter is melted.
• Stir in the rice and mix every 5 minutes on medium heat until the rice is aromatic and the shallots are starting to brown.
• Mix the vegetable stock and the wine together and add to the rice mixture 1 1/2 cups at a time on medium high heat, stirring occasionally when the rice absorbs the liquid.
• Once the rice has absorbed all of the liquid, add the remaining ingredients and simmer until the butter is melted, stirring frequently.

INGREDIENTS

4 cups vegetable stock

1 1/2 cup white wine

2 large shallots (diced)

1 1/2 cups arborio rice

5 tablespoons butter

3 1/2 tablespoons lemon juice

1/2 teaspoon thyme

2 teaspoons bay seasoning

1/4 teaspoon black pepper

1 LB. backfin crab meat

1 teaspoon fresh chopped garlic

ARTICHOKE HEART, SUN DRIED TOMATO , AND JUMBO LUMP BLUE CRAB SAUTÉ

A simple dish packed full of flavor. The sun dried tomatoes and artichoke heart are perfect compliments to one another. Try it mixed with pasta! **SERVES 4-6**

DIRECTIONS

• *In a large sauté pan, heat the olive oil.*
• *Add the onion and sauté until caramelized over medium heat.*
• *Add the artichoke hearts and garlic and sauté for 15 minutes, stirring occasionally.*
• *Add a tablespoon white wine, tomatoes, rosemary, and thyme.*
• *Sauté all until golden brown.*
• *Add the butter, the rest of the wine, lemon juice, and chopped parsley.*
• *Add the jumbo lump crab meat and mix gently.*
• *Let stand for 5 minutes and enjoy.*
• *Optionally add any type of pasta you wish. Fettuccine works quite well.*

INGREDIENTS

1 tablespoon extra virgin olive oil

1 large white onion julienne cut

12 oz. jar quartered artichoke hearts

1 tablespoon chopped garlic

1⁄4 cup white wine plus 1 tablespoon

3⁄4 cup sliced sun dried tomatoes

1⁄4 teaspoon rosemary

1⁄4 teaspoon thyme

1 tablespoon white wine

1 tablespoon lemon juice

1⁄4 cup fresh chopped parsley

1 1⁄2 cup jumbo lump crab meat

85

ALASKAN SNOW CRAB PIZZA

Pizza pizza! This is a unique accompaniment to your favorite game on the TV.
SERVES 2-4

DIRECTIONS

• Preheat oven to 400 degrees.
• Coat the crust evenly with oil.
• Place on a cookie sheet and bake 5 minutes.
• Remove from oven and put a thin coating of béchamel sauce on the crust. (See page 118)
• Add the crab, vegetables and herbs.
• Coat with cheese.
• Bake for 10 minutes then switch the oven to broil.
• Broil until the cheese is melted and browned (2-3 minutes)

INGREDIENTS

1 flat bread pizza crust 9x9

1 red pepper in 1 inch slices

2 small diced tomatoes

2 heaping tablespoons chopped fresh basil

1 tablespoon shredded fresh dill

1 large shallot sliced

2/3 cup shredded snow crab

2/3 cup diced fresh mozzarella

2 tablespoons reggiano parmesan

Salt, pepper, and crushed red pepper to taste

Bechamel sauce

1 tablespoon extra virgin olive oil

SEAFOOD WRAPPED IN PASTRY DOUGH

A flaky dough with a seafood delight inside. More commonly called en chemise. This makes 2. **SERVES 2-4**

DIRECTIONS

• In a medium saucepan, add the oil and shallots and cook until shallots become limp.
• Add the pepper, mushrooms, dill, and artichoke hearts.
• Over medium heat, cook through. About 10 minutes.
• Add the shrimp and cook until the shrimp are pink.
• Add the crab and stir to break up the lumps.
• Add the béchamel sauce (p. 118) and seasonings and keep on low heat.
• Roll out a thawed pastry sheet and place 1/2 the mixture into the center and then do the same for the second one. .
• Fold all edges up, flip and brush it with milk.
• Put on a cookie sheet and place into a 425 degree oven on the top rack for 45 minutes or until golden brown.
• Take out of the oven and let cool for 5 minutes before serving.

INGREDIENTS

8 16/20 ct. shrimp (peeled and deveined cut in half twice)

1 small shallot sliced

1 teaspoon extra virgin olive oil

1 yellow pepper diced

6 button mushrooms chopped

1 teaspoon dill

2/3 cup chopped artichoke hearts

1/2 lb jumbo lump crab meat

Salt and pepper to taste

1/2 teaspoon bay seasoning

1 cup béchamel sauce (p. 118)

2 puff pastry sheets

ROASTED GARLIC AND BUTTER BLUE CRABS

Messy and delightful. These are the go to crabs when you want something untraditional. Sweet and moist. **SERVES 2**

DIRECTIONS

• In a heavy skillet on high heat, place the crabs, garlic, and 1 stick butter in and cover for 5 minutes until the garlic is golden brown.
• Add the rest of the ingredients and cover on medium low heat for about 20 minutes, or until the crabs are cooked through. Flipping the crabs and stirring every 5 minutes.

INGREDIENTS

4 large crabs split and cleaned of the gills and mustard

1/4 cup fresh chopped garlic

2 sticks of unsalted butter (1 cup)

1 tablespoon parsley

1/2 teaspoon bay seasoning

SHRIMP QUESADILLA

The perfect snack for a fiesta night. The flavor comes from the seasoning.
Fill it with anything you like, but these tender shrimp are sure to please.
SERVES 2-4

DIRECTIONS

• Add the first 6 ingredients into a coffee grinder and grind until smooth or pulverize with a mortar and pestle.
• Place the next 6 ingredients plus the seasoning mix (to taste) into a medium sauté pan over medium heat and cover.
• Cook until the shrimp are done and the onions are soft.
• Coat large skillet with a little bit of oil and place over medium high heat and place 1 of the tortilla shells in the pan.
• Add 1⁄2 of the cheese and the remaining cooked ingredients.
• Place the rest of the cheese on top with the cilantro and tomatoes.
• Cover with the other tortilla shell.
• Let the bottom shell cook for about 5 minutes and then flip over and cook until both are browned and the cheese is melted.

INGREDIENTS

1 tablespoon annatto seed

1⁄2 teaspoon black peppercorn

2 cloves

1 teaspoon cumin seed

1⁄2 teaspoon smoked paprika

1⁄2 teaspoon chili powder

Juice of 1 lime

12 jumbo shrimp (quartered)

1⁄4 cup thinly sliced onion

1 tablespoon garlic

2/3 cup roasted red pepper

1⁄2 of the seasoning mix

2 flour tortilla shells

1 1⁄2 cup thinly slice cheddar from the block

2 small diced tomatoes

1/3 cup chopped cilantro

SNOW CRAB AND VEGE-TABLE OMELET

Breakfast is served with this easy omelet loaded with veggies and crab meat.
SERVES 2

DIRECTIONS

• Heat a large sauté pan and coat with a non stick cooking spray.
• Over medium high heat, add the eggs.
• Add the rest of the ingredients and turn down to medium low.
• Cover the pan.
• Check often until the eggs are firm.
• Gently fold to make an omelet.

INGREDIENTS

6 eggs (beaten)

1/4 cup parsley

1 1/2 tablespoons red onion

1/4 cup diced red pepper

1/4 cup diced sun dried tomatoes

1/4 cup chopped spinach

Salt, pepper, and bay seasoning to taste

1/3 cup jumbo lump crab meat (lightly shredded)

SHRIMP SCAMPI

This simple, timeless dish is a breeze to make. Serve this over angel hair pasta, or on its own. **SERVES 2**

DIRECTIONS

• Heat pan with medium heat.
• Simmer all ingredients, flipping shrimp occasionally until bubbling and shrimp are cooked through (about 10 minutes).

INGREDIENTS

1/2 cup white wine

1 tablespoon chopped garlic

1 tablespoon lemon juice

2 tablespoons unsalted butter

1/4 cup fresh parsley

12 peeled and deveined shrimp (16/20 ct.)

SAUTÉED SOFT SHELL CRABS

Some people love these fried, but for a new mouth-watering way to enjoy softshell crabs give this recipe a try. Simple, pure, delicious! **SERVES 1-2**

DIRECTIONS

• Prepare soft shell crabs for cooking according to instructions on page 13.
• Heat pan on medium high heat.
• Add all the ingredients except the crabs and cook until butter is melted.
• Then add the soft shell crabs and cook 7 minutes on each side.
• Reduce heat to a simmer and cook another 5 minutes.

INGREDIENTS

3 tablespoons clarified butter

1 tablespoon chopped garlic

1/4 cup chopped parsley

1/2 teaspoon crushed red pepper

1/4 cup lemon juice

1/4 cup white wine

2 - 6 inch soft shell crabs

CRAB QUICHE

Perfect for a lazy Sunday brunch. Make the night before and reheat for an even lazier Sunday morning. **SERVES 4-6**

DIRECTIONS

- Preheat oven at 400 degrees.
- Pre-cook pie shell for 10 minutes in oven.
- Stir all ingredients together except the parmesan cheese.
- Place the mixture in the pie shell.
- Sprinkle with the cheese.
- Bake in the oven for 35-40 minutes or until the middle is firm.

INGREDIENTS

4 eggs beaten

1/2 cup heavy cream

1/4 cup chopped chives

1 tablespoon chopped fresh dill

1/4 cup marscapone cheese

1 cup jumbo lump crab meat

1/2 teaspoon bay seasoning

Salt and pepper to taste

Reggiano parmesan

1 - 9 inch pie shell

Jumbo Lump Crab Cakes

A personal favorite! These are a perennial crowd pleaser! **SERVES 4-6**

DIRECTIONS

- Whisk the eggs and mayonnaise together.
- Add in the mustard, garlic, onions, lemon zest, bay seasoning and whisk together.
- Fold in the backfin crab meat and the bread crumbs until everything is mixed together well.
- Gently add the jumbo lump crab meat.
- Preheat oven to 350 degrees.
- Form into 5 oz. cakes.
- Lightly dust them with bread crumbs and paprika.
- Bake them for 15 minutes and then turn your oven to broil.
- Drizzle melted butter on top of the crab cakes and cook another 6 minutes.

INGREDIENTS

2 eggs

2 tablespoons mayonnaise

1 tablespoon Dijon mustard

1 teaspoon fresh chopped garlic

1/3 cup diced spring onions

1 tablespoon lemon zest

1 tablespoon bay seasoning

1 LB. backfin crab meat

1 LB. jumbo lump crab meat

2 tablespoons bread crumbs + extra to top off crab cakes

Paprika

Melted butter

FRIED SOFT SHELL CRABS

From a sandwich to a main coarse, the possibilities are endless. Nice and crunchy, these are sure to please every crab lover. **SERVES 2-6**

DIRECTIONS

• Prepare soft shell crabs for cooking according to instructions on page 13.
• Mix the first 6 ingredients in a large bowl and set aside.
• Beat the eggs.
• Place the flour into another bowl.
• Heat your fryer or place oil into a sauté pan 1 inch deep until it reaches 350 degrees.
• Coat the crabs with the flour and then transfer to the eggs 1 at a time.
• Coat with the other dry ingredients until evenly covered.
• Fry until golden brown on both sides (about 5-7 minutes each side).

INGREDIENTS

1 box of your favorite batter

3/4 cup cornmeal

1 tablespoon chopped parsley

1 teaspoon paprika

2 tablespoons maple sugar

1 tablespoon bay seasoning

8 eggs

3 cups flour

4-6 soft shell crabs

Canola oil

LOBSTER NEWBERG

Serve over toasted bread. The creaminess and rich flavor is what makes this dish stand out. **SERVES 2-4**

DIRECTIONS

• Sauté the lobster and butter together until butter is melted.
• Add the 2 tablespoons sherry and brandy and cook over medium heat for 2 minutes.
• Take the lobster meat out with a slotted spoon, reserving the juices in the pan. -
• Add the heavy cream and bring to a boil until reduced to about 1 cup.
• Stir in the remainder of the sherry and brandy, nutmeg and salt cooking over low heat for 5 minutes.
• Take off the heat and add the 3 beaten egg yolks, paprika, and crushed red pepper until it makes a creamy sauce.
• Add in the lobster meat, stir, and serve over toast

INGREDIENTS

2 cups cooked lobster cut into 3/4 inch pieces

1/4 cup butter

2 tablespoons sherry + 1 teaspoon

2 tablespoons brandy + 1 teaspoon

1 3/4 cup heavy cream

1/4 teaspoon nutmeg

Salt to taste

Pinch of paprika

Pinch of crushed red pepper

3 beaten egg yolks

LITTLENECK CLAMS WITH CHORIZO

A warming hearty dish with potatoes and lots of flavor. You could serve this over pasta or let it stand alone. Pass the bread please! **SERVES 2-4**

DIRECTIONS

- *In a large sauté pan heat the oil.*
- *Add the onions, peppers, and potatoes.*
- *Cook on medium heat for 20 minutes, stirring occasionally.*
- *Add the chorizo and cook for 15 minutes covered stirring occasionally.*
- *Add the white wine, clams, and salt and pepper.*
- *Cook covered until all of the clams pop open. About 10 minutes.*
- *Add the cilantro and toss over pasta, or place on a large plate to serve.*

INGREDIENTS

1 large sliced onion

1 yellow pepper cut into 1 inch strips

1 red pepper cut into 1 inch strips

2 medium sized red potatoes (diced)

1/4 cup extra virgin olive oil

2 cups sliced chorizo

1/2 cup white wine

24 littleneck clams

1/4 cup cilantro

Salt and pepper to taste

JAMAICAN JERK SHRIMP

This definitely warms the soul. Pair it with white rice for a complete meal. The sweet yet spicy combination is something to talk about and something you are sure to crave. **SERVES 2**

DIRECTIONS

- Heat the butter in a sauté pan on medium heat.
- Add the first 5 ingredients to the pan and sauté until the shallots are soft (approx. 7 minutes).
- Add the rest of the ingredients and simmer for 10 minutes.

INGREDIENTS

12 peeled and deveined shrimp (16-20 ct.)

3⁄4 cups sliced shallots

1/3 cup diced sun-dried tomatoes

1/3 cup chopped celery

1/3 cup chopped cilantro

2 tablespoons butter

1/3 cup vinegar

1 tablespoon chopped garlic

1 cup sliced okra

1 1⁄2 tablespoons Jamaican jerk seasoning

BRICKER'S CIOPPINO

This is a perfect go-to seafood dish. It has an authentic rustic taste and is for those who aren't afraid to get their hands dirty. Work is involved, but the outcome and love are well worth it. Serve with a lot of bread of coarse!
SERVES 6-8

DIRECTIONS

• From the live state, take off the top shell of the blue crab and discard the mustard and gills. Wash them thoroughly and split in half.
• In a cast iron dutch oven or large saucepan heat the oil on medium heat until it's hot.
• Add the onion and garlic and sauté until onions are soft.
• Add the tomatoes, clam juice, parsley, crushed red pepper, bay seasoning, water, and white pepper.
• Lower your heat until it's simmering.
• Add the blue crabs, cover on medium low heat for about 45 minutes, making sure the crab is submersed.
• Add the shrimp and split the lobster tails in half and add them, stir and cover for another 10 minutes.
• Next add the clams and cover for another 10 minutes, stirring occasionally until all the clams are open.
• Reduce heat to low and let on the stove until you are ready to serve.

INGREDIENTS

6 large blue crabs

1 LB shrimp (16-20 ct) shell on

4 - 4 oz. lobster tails

24 littleneck clams

1/4 cup extra virgin olive oil

1 large white onion (julienne cut)

6 garlic cloves sliced

1 cup white wine

6 large tomatoes diced with the juices

1 8oz. jar clam juice

1/2 cup fresh parsley

Pinch crushed red pepper

1 tablespoon bay seasoning

1 1/2 cup water

1 teaspoon white pepper

BAKED OYSTER PIE

Have any leftover oysters? Try this out for a great dinner any day of the week!
SERVES 4-6

DIRECTIONS

- Preheat oven to 400 degrees.
- Add the onion, celery, mushrooms, and butter in a skillet on medium heat.
- Sauté until the onions are clear.
- Add the garlic and milk on medium high heat until bubbling.
- Mix melted butter and flour to form roux.
- Add the roux and simmer until you get the moderately thick consistency.
- Follow the directions to heat the pie shell.
- Place the ingredients into the shell and cover with the puffed pastry dough.
- Brush the pie with milk.
- Bake until golden brown (about 25 minutes).

INGREDIENTS

1 small onion (julienne cut)

2 large button mushrooms (chopped)

3 tablespoons unsalted butter

1 cup diced celery

1 teaspoon garlic

1 can evaporated milk (5 oz.)

1 pint shucked oysters

Salt and pepper to taste

4 Tablespoons melted butter

6 Tablespoons flour

1 9 inch pie shell

1 Sheet puffed pastry dough

Milk

SAUCES

COCKTAIL SAUCE

Lets kick up the heat a little bit! Nothing goes better with shrimp and crab cakes than a really good cocktail sauce. This has a really nice sweet and tangy taste with the touch of heat at the end to bring it all together.

BECHAMÉL SAUCE

A classic sauce with a large range of versatility.

MORNAY SAUCE

This is a nice creamy addition to your stuffed mushrooms. Top them off and bake according to the recipe. But don't stop there, this can be baked on top of any crab dish for that extra creaminess.

DIRECTIONS

• Mix all ingredients in a bowl and serve.

• Double up for a party!

INGREDIENTS

1 cup ketchup

5 shakes smoked chipotle Tabasco sauce

1⁄2 teaspoon Worcestershire sauce

1⁄2 teaspoon diced garlic

1 tablespoon lemon juice

2 tablespoons horseradish

2 teaspoons Jamaican jerk seasoning

DIRECTIONS

• Melt the butter in a heavy saucepan over medium heat.
• Add the flour and stir to make a roux.
• Slowly stir in the milk while whisking until creamy.
• Take off the heat and add the seasonings.

INGREDIENTS

1 stick of butter (1⁄2 cup)

Salt and white pepper to taste

1/3 cup flour

2 1⁄2 cups whole milk

1⁄4 teaspoon nutmeg

Pinch of onion powder

DIRECTIONS

• Mix all ingredients in a bowl.

INGREDIENTS

1 egg

3⁄4 cup grated Parmesan cheese

1⁄2 cup mayonnaise

3⁄4 tablespoon Dijon mustard

1 tablespoon lemon juice

HOLLANDAISE SAUCE

This golden sauce is like the nectar of the gods and is surprisingly simple to make from scratch. You can place this on vegetables, eggs, crab meat, the possibilities are limitless. This makes a great topping for our Bacon Wrapped Lobster!

REMOULADE SAUCE

This is a go to sauce for pretty much everything seafood. It's light and a little bit tangy. Lets just say tartar sauce doesn't even stand a chance next to this.

SPICY HONEY-CHIPOTLE SAUCE

What makes this sauce pop is the extra heat with the sweet. Perfect for our corn fritters. This could also be a glaze for any type of meat or mild fish.

DIRECTIONS

• In a medium saucepan, bring 1 inch of water to a simmer.
• Put egg yolks and lemon juice in a medium sized bowl and whisk over the simmering water.
• Whisking constantly, slowly add the butter until smooth and incorporated.
• Remove from heat and add salt and pepper.
• For a thinner sauce, add more butter.
• Serve sauce hot.

INGREDIENTS

1 1/2 cup hot melted unsalted butter

6 egg yolks

1/4 cup lemon juice

Pinch of salt and white pepper

DIRECTIONS

• Mix all the ingredients in a bowl and serve chilled.

INGREDIENTS

1 cup mayo

1/3 cup diced green pepper

1/3 cup diced red pepper

1 teaspoon Dijon mustard

2 tablespoons chili sauce

1 teaspoon smoked chipotle Tabasco sauce

1 teaspoon chopped garlic

1 teaspoon lemon juice

1/2 teaspoon chili powder

2 tablespoons fresh chopped parsley

1/2 teaspoon bay seasoning

DIRECTIONS

• The chipotle peppers are the kind you can get in a can at the grocery store.
• Finely chop the peppers and add with the other ingredients into a medium sauce pan.
• Bring to a simmer until reduced (20 minutes).

INGREDIENTS

1/4 cup chipotle peppers

1 cup honey

1/2 teaspoon chopped garlic

1/4 cup diced shallots

1/3 cup vinegar

4 tablespoons maple sugar

1/2 cup water

DESSERTS

ESPRESSO BROWNIES

A chocolaty pick me up. Best served warm with a cold glass of milk.

DIRECTIONS

- Preheat oven to 325 degrees.
- Grease an 8x8 inch pan.
- In a bowl, combine the flour and baking soda and set aside.
- In another bowl, combine the brown and cane sugars.
- Mix together and blend in the butter to make a paste.
- Melt the chocolate in a double boiler and add to the sugar batter.
- Combine the espresso into the boiling water to dissolve and add it to the sugar batter.
- Beat until smooth.
- Add the eggs and the vanilla and almond extract.
- Add the flour mixture and the chocolate chips.
- Blend just until everything is combined.
- Pour into the greased pan and bake for 35 minutes or until a toothpick inserted into the center comes out clean.

OR

- Pour into small muffin tins for 25-30 minutes or until toothpick comes out clean.
- Once cooled place chocolate covered espresso beans in the center of each brownie.

INGREDIENTS

2 1/2 cups flour

1/2 teaspoon baking soda

1 cup dark brown sugar

1/2 cup pure cane sugar

1 cup unsalted butter (melted)

2.5 ounces unsweetened baking chocolate

1 tablespoon ground espresso

1 tablespoon water

2 large eggs

1 teaspoon pure vanilla extract

1 teaspoon almond extract

1 cup chocolate chips

1 package chocolate covered espresso beans

BLACK RASPBERRY COBBLER

Sit back, relax, and let the cobbler do the talking. You will be the hero next time someone says bring dessert. That's if you can ever let it go! This is also a wonderful way to use those fresh picked wild raspberries at the beginning of the summer.

DIRECTIONS

- Preheat oven to 375 degrees.
- Place the first 4 ingredients into a bowl and let sit out, stirring occasionally, for about an hour.
- Place into a 9x9 inch baking pan
- Mix together the flour, baking powder, and sugar into a separate bowl.
- Add the butter and stir in with a fork until it forms crumbs.
- Add the heavy cream and continue folding the ingredients together until it makes a dough.
- It will seem a little dry, this is good!
- Knead the dough until it forms a ball, and knead once more, pushing the air pockets out.
- Place on top of your berry mixture and brush with heavy cream.
- Bake about 45 minutes or until the topping is golden brown and the center is bubbling.

INGREDIENTS

Filling

6 cups black raspberries

1 cup sugar

2 1/2 tablespoons cornstarch

1/4 teaspoon salt

Topping

1 3/4 cup flour

1 3/4 teaspoon baking powder

1/4 cup sugar

6 tablespoons butter (chopped)

3/4 cup heavy cream

NEW YORK STYLE CHEESECAKE

A classic dessert. Feel free to add any toppings you wish!

DIRECTIONS

• Mix the first 3 ingredients together and press into the bottom and 2 inches up the sides of a 9 inch spring form pan. Place in the freezer.
• With a blender, mix the cream cheese until whipped.
• Add the sugar, cornstarch, and vanilla extract until blended through.
• Add the eggs and beat until well incorporated.
• Stir in the sour cream.
• Place the mixture in the crust.
• Put the cake in a preheated oven set at 325 degrees for about an hour and 15 minutes.
• Take out of the oven and let sit for 20 minutes.
• Loosen the side of the pan and let sit out for another hour.
• Place in your refrigerator for at least 4 hours.
• Take out of the pan and serve!

INGREDIENTS

2 1/2 cups smashed graham cracker crumbs

1/2 cup + 1 tablespoon melted butter

2 tablespoons sugar

4 packages (8 oz. each) cream cheese

1 1/3 cup sugar

1 1/2 tablespoons cornstarch

1 tablespoon vanilla extract

3 eggs

1 cup sour cream

GRASSHOPPER PIE

Definitely a personal favorite. Cool and refreshing, a must have for warm summer nights.

DIRECTIONS

• Crush the cookies and place in a bowl.
• Add the chocolate and the butter on low heat until the chocolate is melted.
• Mix in with the crushed cookies and mold onto the bottom of a 9 inch spring form pan.
• Place it into your freezer.
• On the stove in a small pot, add the marshmallows and milk on low heat until the marshmallows are melted through.
• Mix in the crème de menthe and crème de cacao.
• Let cool.
• In a separate bowl add the heavy cream and whip until the cream holds soft peaks.
• Add the marshmallow mix slowly while whisking until incorporated.
• Place on top of the cookie shell in the spring form pan.
• Top with a little more cookie crumbs and shaved chocolate.
• Place in freezer overnight.

INGREDIENTS

30 cream filled chocolate cookies

2 oz. 60% chocolate

3 Tablespoons butter

3 cups mini marshmallows

1/2 cup whole milk

1/4 cup crème de menthe

1/4 cup crème de cacao

1 1/2 cup heavy cream

ORANGE SORBET

Refreshing, packed with flavor, this is definitely the go to recipe for what you're craving on a hot summers day. But by all means, don't stop with summer!

DIRECTIONS

- Squeeze the oranges through a colander into a medium size pot.
- Throw in 2 oranges that you just squeezed into the pot.
- Add the water and sugar.
- Heat on low heat for about 45 minutes.
- Pour into a bowl, cover, and refrigerate until cold.
- Place into your ice cream maker and follow the manufactures instructions.
- Can be eaten right away or stored in an air tight container in the freezer.

INGREDIENTS

15 Large oranges

1 cup water

1 cup raw sugar (turbinado)

FRESH MINT ICE CREAM

The fresh mint and cream make this a family favorite. Easy to make and hard to put down.

DIRECTIONS

• Slowly heat the milk, half and half, and mint leaves until it reaches about 180 degrees. Being careful not to let it come to a boil.
• Remove from the heat and let stand for 20 minutes.
• Pour the mixture into a bowl through a colander and squeeze the mint into the mixture.
• In another bowl, combine the sugar, salt, and egg yolk.
• Stir with a fork for about 5 minutes.
• Add half of the cream mixture and mix until sugar is melted.
• Put the remaining cream mixture into a pot and then add the cream/sugar mixture.
• Cook over low heat until it comes to 160 degrees.
• Pour it into a bowl and stir in the vanilla and green food coloring.
• Place it into the refrigerator, covered, stirring often until the mixture is completely cooled.
• Put it into your ice cream maker and follow the manufacturer's instructions.
• Place the mixture into an airtight container overnight for a firmer ice cream. Let sit out 10 minutes before serving.

INGREDIENTS

4 cups whole milk

2 cups half and half

40-45 fresh mint leaves

4 egg yolks

1 1/2 cup raw sugar (turbinado)

Very small pinch of salt

1 1/2 teaspoons real vanilla extract

10 drops green food coloring

135

Jeremy Bricker, Executive Chef, Harbour House Crabs - Always fascinated by the complex designs and artistry of what was on my plate, I started at a very young age transforming whatever could be found in the kitchen into a nice meal. As soon as I was old enough I started dedicating my time to learning as much as I could about cooking and the food industry.

Additionally, being raised near the Eastern Shore, I was always drawn to the ocean and her bays. The raw power combined with the peaceful calmness of the sea took my breath away. Whether surfing or just hanging out with friends, I was at the beach or by the Chesapeake every chance I had. I vividly remember my first crab feast and crack'n one open as I sat at a table covered in paper and dozens of freshly steamed crabs surrounded by family and friends. After eating as much shell as crab, a kind gentleman came over and showed me the "proper" way to eat a blue crab. From that day on, I was hooked on the savory seasoning and sweet taste of crab combined with the rich tradition of gathering with loved ones or strangers that were soon to be old friends.

I would like to thank my family and friends for their constant support and always asking me to cook for them. Without that silly annoyance, I would not be where I am today. These experiences early on along with my continued passion for cooking and the taste of the sea have inspired these recipes. My hope is that you will enjoy sharing them with your family and friends to create your own special memories.

Tom Wenger - Tom is a freelance photographer who has photographed all over the United States. While he works with many photographic subjects, food photography is of particular interest to him. He is drawn to the challenges that each new dish poses and rarely resorts to the "tricks of the trade" to get the shot, preferring rather to shoot real food in real environments. What that means to you the reader is that you know that you too can attain the results found photographed in this book. All of this food was ready to eat (and often was when the shoot was finished). Rest assured that the photographer was quite impressed with the recipes and Chef Bricker's innate ability to compliment the delicate shellfish with complex flavors.

HARBOURHOUSE CRABS™

WWW.ILOVECRABS.COM or (888) 458 8272

"Our Treat"

We'd be delighted if you'd care to share "iLoveCrabs" with friends, neighbors, club members and fellow chefs. We hope you share the same passion and excitement for crabs as we do. If you - or friends desire to learn more about Harbour House Crabs, simply visit www.iLoveCrabs.com. Have a story to share? We'd love to hear it.